E.P.L.

D0793681

Going Green at School

Molly Aloian

Crabtree Publishing Company
www.crabtreebooks.com

Author
Molly Aloian

Publishing plan research and development
Reagan Miller

Editor
Rachel Eagen

Proofreader and indexer
Wendy Scavuzzo

Design
Samara Parent

Photo research
Samara Parent

Production coordinator and prepress technician
Samara Parent

Print coordinator
Margaret Amy Salter

Photographs
Bigstockphoto: page 3
istockphoto: page 21
Thinkstock: title page, pages 4, 15, 18
All other images by Shutterstock

Library and Archives Canada Cataloguing in Publication

Aloian, Molly, author
       Going green at school / Molly Aloian.

(The green scene)
Includes index.
Issued in print and electronic formats.
ISBN 978-0-7787-0264-1 (bound).--ISBN 978-0-7787-0283-2
(pbk.).--ISBN 978-1-4271-1268-2 (pdf).--ISBN 978-1-4271-9437-4
(html)

       1. School buildings--Environmental aspects--Juvenile literature.
2. Waste minimization--Juvenile literature. 3. Recycling (Waste, etc.)--
Juvenile literature. I. Title.

LB3241.A56 2013   j371.6   C2013-905209-7
                                             C2013-905210-0

Library of Congress Cataloging-in-Publication Data

Aloian, Molly.
 Going green at school / Molly Aloian.
   pages cm. -- (The green scene)
 Includes index.
 ISBN 978-0-7787-0264-1 (reinforced library binding) -- ISBN 978-0-7787-
0283-2 (pbk.) -- ISBN 978-1-4271-1268-2 (electronic pdf) -- ISBN 978-1-4271-
9437-4 (electronic html)
 1. Environmentalism--Juvenile literature. 2. Environmental education--
Juvenile literature. I. Title.

 GE195.5.A47 2013
 370.28'6--dc23

                    2013030081

Crabtree Publishing Company

Printed in Canada/092013/BF20130815

www.crabtreebooks.com   1-800-387-7650

Copyright © **2014 CRABTREE PUBLISHING COMPANY**. All rights reserved. No part of this publication may be reproduced, stored in a retrieval system or be transmitted in any form or by any means, electronic, mechanical, photocopying, recording, or otherwise, without the prior written permission of Crabtree Publishing Company. In Canada: We acknowledge the financial support of the Government of Canada through the Canada Book Fund for our publishing activities.

Published in Canada
Crabtree Publishing
616 Welland Ave.
St. Catharines, Ontario
L2M 5V6

Published in the United States
Crabtree Publishing
PMB 59051
350 Fifth Avenue, 59th Floor
New York, New York 10118

Published in the United Kingdom
Crabtree Publishing
Maritime House
Basin Road North, Hove
BN41 1WR

Published in Australia
Crabtree Publishing
3 Charles Street
Coburg North
VIC 3058

Contents

Going green

Have you heard the saying "going green"? What do you think that means? Going green means trying to lessen our **impact** on Earth. To lessen our impact, we must make small changes in our lives, at home, and at school.

Huge areas of forest are cut down every day to make enough paper for you to use at school.

Helping Earth every day

We can take better care of Earth by **conserving** energy, using less **natural resources**, cleaning up the environment, and preventing **pollution**.

Take Action!

Trees are an important natural resource. Paper and wood come from trees. How can you help save and protect trees?

Getting to school

Black exhaust from vehicles pollutes the air, causes health problems, and increases **global warming**.

How do you get to and from school every day? Cars, trucks, and buses need energy to get from place to place. Most of this energy comes from burning **fossil fuels**, such as oil, gas, and coal. Burning fossil fuels causes pollution.

Preventing pollution

You can help reduce pollution by riding your bike, rollerblading, skateboarding, or walking to and from school. You can reduce air pollution even more by encouraging your friends to do the same!

Take Action!

Participate in International Walk to School Day on October 9. Kids from all over the world walk to and from school on this day each year.

Create a green classroom

Your classroom is a great place to start going green at school. On bright sunny days, keep classroom lights off and use natural light. You will help save energy and burn fewer fossil fuels.

Many schools in the United States spend a lot of money on energy. This money could instead be used to buy more books for classrooms and libraries.

Take Action!

*Water-based paints, **biodegradable** pens, acid-free glue sticks, and pencils made of recycled wood are all environmentally friendly school supplies. How many of these supplies are used in your school?*

Get unplugged

Did you know that computers and other appliances use electricity even when they are not on? Save energy by unplugging televisions and other equipment in your classroom when they are not in use.

Pass on paper

As you read the words on this page, a forest about the size of a football field is being cut down to make paper. In the United States, people use more than 30 million tons (27 million metric tons) of printing and writing paper each year.

Write on the back of test papers to reuse them instead of throwing them away. Ask your teacher to start a scrap paper bin in your classroom.

Make sure your notebooks are made from recycled paper.

Saving and reuse

Saving and reusing paper at school is a great way to help the environment. Use good-on-one-side (GOOS) paper for doodling, rough work, and taking notes.

Part with plastic bottles

Making plastic water bottles creates dangerous **greenhouse gases**, which adds to global warming on Earth. Americans throw away 2.5 million plastic bottles every hour. These plastic bottles take hundreds of years to break down in **landfills**.

Plastic water bottles are bad for the environment. They cause pollution and some never break down.

No plastic

Make your school a "no plastic bottle" zone. Bring a reusable water bottle to school instead of using plastic bottles. You will help prevent global warming and keep plastic bottles out of landfills.

You can refill your reusable water bottle and bring it to school every day.

13

Litter-free lunches

Many lunch foods and snack foods are wrapped in packaging that ends up in landfills. In fact, each person in the United States sends over 250 pounds (133 kilograms) of packaging to landfills every year.

Never bring your lunch to school in a plastic or paper bag. Always use a cloth or reusable bag and reusable containers for your lunch.

Lunch without litter

Try to pack a litter-free lunch every day. Use a lunch box with sections and a reusable bottle for juice or water. Try to avoid juice boxes and other packaging that will end up in a landfill. Bring metal utensils and a cloth napkin for your lunch. These items can be washed rather than thrown away.

Create compost

Compost is a mixture of waste, such as dead leaves, vegetable peels, and fruit cores, which has broken down and changed into rich soil. The soil is full of **nutrients** that help plants grow.

Compost can be spread around flowers, tomatoes, and vegetable plants to help them grow and stay healthy.

Breaking down

Compost bins can be used at your school to recycle food waste from student lunches and the cafeteria. The waste will break down inside the bin with the help of worms, flies, and other **decomposers**. In about six to nine months, the waste will start to look and smell like dark brown soil.

Do you know what items can go into a compost bin? Use books and the Internet to find out.

Remember the three Rs

The three Rs are Reduce, Reuse, and Recycle. They are important to remember as you go green at school. Reducing means throwing away less garbage. Can the items you use at school be reused or recycled?

Millions of children around the world cannot afford school supplies, clothes, or other items. Instead of throwing away your old things, give them to someone else who can use them.

Reuse, reduce, recycle

Reuse last year's backpack and school supplies instead of buying new ones. This will reduce the amount of garbage you throw away. Recycle last year's school work or reuse it as scrap paper. If you have grown out of your old school clothes, donate them instead of throwing them away.

Take Action!

Start a student-run recycling club at your school. Make sure everyone at your school recycles plastic, paper, metal, and glass.

You could decorate your old backpack with buttons or patches to make it feel like new.

Earth-friendly field trips

If you think garbage just disappears, it is time for your school to take a field trip to a landfill to see where our garbage ends up. There may also be an alternative energy plant near your school. This is a great place to learn about **renewable resources**, such as sun, wind, and water.

Taking a field trip to a wind farm can help you understand how electricity can be made from the wind.

A tour of a local recycling center is another great field trip. You will learn how plastic can be turned into park benches and how paper is recycled.

Take Action!

*Ask a teacher to help you and your classmates grow a class garden. You can grow vegetables or flowers. Use compost to **fertilize** your garden.*

These students are on a tour at a recycling center. They are learning what items can be recycled.

Earth events

There are several environmental events throughout the year that bring awareness to Earth's problems. Research the events on the Internet and mark them on your calendar. Plan activities that you can do on these days to take care of Earth.

On April 22, over one billion people take part in Earth Day to help protect Earth. People plant trees, pick up garbage, and remind others to reduce, reuse, and recycle.

Learning more

Books

Barraclough, Sue. *Be an Eco Hero at School.* Sea to Sea Publications, 2013.

Domnauer, Teresa. *Ready, Set, Go Green! Eco-Friendly Activities for School and Home.* Frank Schaffer Publications, 2009.

Gaarder-Juntti, Oona. *What in the World Is a Green School?* Super Sandcastle, 2010.

Johnson, J. Angelique. *The Eco-Student's Guide to Being Green at School.* Picture Window Books, 2010.

Websites

Green School
http://www.greenschool.org/

Eco-Schools
http://www.eco-schools.org/

Green Your School
http://www.dosomething.org/green-your-school

Greencyclopedia: How to Go Green at School
http://gogreencyclopedia.blogspot.ca/2012/12/how-to-go-green-at-school.html

23

Words to know

Note: Some boldfaced words are defined where they appear in the book.

biodegradable (bahy-oh-di-GREY-duh-buhl) adjective Describing something that can break down naturally

conserve (kuhn-SURV) verb To use carefully or keep safe

decomposers (dee-kuhm-POH-zers) noun Living things, such as worms, flies or millipedes, that can break down waste

fertilize (FUR-tl-ahyz) verb To add substances to soil to make plants grow

fossil fuels (FOS-uhl FYOO-uhlz) noun Fuels such as oil, natural gas, and coal that are used to power cars, make electricity, and heat and cool homes

global warming (GLOH-buhl WAWRM-ing) noun The gradual increase in Earth's temperature

greenhouse gases (GREEN-hous GAS-ez) noun Harmful gases that remain trapped in Earth's atmosphere

impact (im-PAKT) noun A strong or forceful effect

landfills (LAND-filz) noun Huge holes in the ground that are filled with garbage and then covered with soil

natural resources (NACH-er-uhl REE-sawrs-ez) noun Useful materials, such as trees and water, that are found in nature

nutrients (NOO-tree-uhnts) noun Natural substances that help living things grow and stay healthy

pollution (puh-LOO-shuhn) noun Chemicals, fumes, waste, or garbage that harm or spoil Earth

renewable resources (ri-NOO-EY-buhl REE-sawrs-ez) noun Sun, wind, water, and other materials from nature that are able to be replaced

A *noun* is a person, place, or thing.
An *adjective* is a word that tells you what something is like.
A *verb* is an action word that tells you what someone or something does.

Index